Sherwood Middle School
Media Center
Shrewsbury, Massachusetts

Across the Solar System

Rod Theodorou

Heinemann Library
Chicago, Illinois

Designed by **AMR**

Printed by Wing King Tong, in Hong Kong

04 03 02 01 00
10 9 8 7 6 5 4 3 2 1

Library of Congress Cataloging-in-Publication Data
Theodorou, Rod.
　　Across the solar system / Rod Theodorou.
　　　　p. cm. – (Amazing journeys)
　　Includes bibliographical references and index.
　　Summary: Takes the reader on a journey through the solar system,
describing comets, asteroids, and the planets, including their
average temperature, length of day, distance from the sun, and more.
　　ISBN 1-57572-486-3 (library binding)
　　1. Solar system Juvenile literature. [1. Solar system.
2. Planets.] I. Title. II. Series: Telford, Carole, 1961-
Amazing journeys.
QB501.3.T48 2000
523.2—dc21　　　　　　　　　99-37162
　　　　　　　　　　　　　　CIP

Acknowledgments
The Publishers would like to thank the following for permission to reproduce photographs:

Oxford Scientific Films/NASA, pp. 16, 17; Science Photo Library/European Space Agency, p. 10; Science Photo Library/Ludek Pesek, p. 23; Science Photo Library/Mehau Kulyk, p. 11; Science Photo Library/NASA, pp. 13, 14, 15, 17, 19, 20, 21, 22, 24, 25, 26, 27; Science Photo Library/ National Optical Astronomy Observatories, p. 11; Science Photo Library/US Geological Survey, pp. 12, 18; Science Photo Library/ Victor Habbick Visions, p. 6.

Cover photograph reproduced with permission of Bruce Coleman Collection.

Every effort has been made to contact copyright holders of any material reproduced in this book. Any omissions will be rectified in subsequent printings if notice is given to the Publisher.

Some words are shown in bold, **like this.**
You can find out what they mean by looking in the glossary

Contents

Introduction 6

Journey Map 8

The Blazing Sun 10

Mercury–the Dead World 12

Venus–Our Savage Sister 14

Earth–the Water Planet 16

Mars–the Red Planet 18

Jupiter–the Gas Giant 20

Saturn–the Ringed Planet 22

Uranus–the Green Planet 24

Neptune–the Blue Planet 25

Pluto–the Mystery Planet 26

Exploring Space–Planet Probe 27

Glossary *28*

Space Calendar *30*

More Books to Read *31*

Index *32*

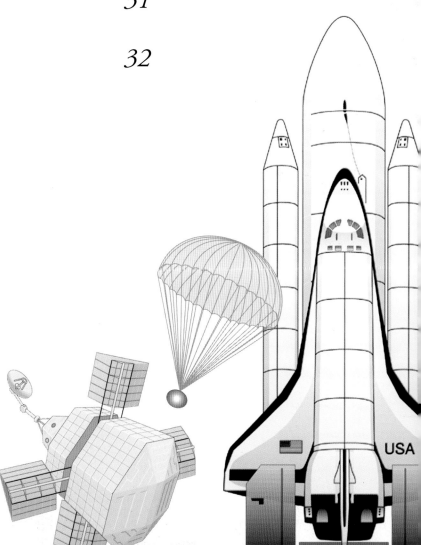

Introduction

You are about to go on an amazing journey. You are going to climb inside a spaceship, more advanced than any that exists today. You are going to travel to the center of our **solar system**, across millions of miles, to witness the blazing fury of our spectacular sun. Then you are going to travel away from the sun, across silent, cold, black space. You are going to visit each of our solar system's nine planets, from the dead, colorless world of Mercury, to the dazzling, rainbow storm clouds of Jupiter.

As you visit each planet, you will learn how very different they are and how precious our own planet is—the only planet in the solar system that can support millions of life forms.

1. Sun
2. Mercury
3. Venus
4. Earth
5. Mars
6. Jupiter
7. Saturn
8. Uranus
9. Neptune
10. Pluto

The first four, or inner, planets are small, rocky worlds. Four of the outer planets are gas giants—huge balls of gases and liquids. Pluto is the smallest and farthest planet from the sun.

Outer planets

Inner planets

All the planets in our solar system move around the sun (*solar* means of the sun). The sun is a massive ball of exploding gases called a **star**. There are billions of other stars in our **galaxy**. Some of them also have planets **orbiting** in their own solar systems.

Our spaceship is designed to travel at incredible speed. Its **hull** can withstand crushing **pressures,** as well as intense heat and cold. We are going to need it, because we are going to explore places where no one has set foot. What will they be like? Could they support other forms of life?

The spaceship's engines fire up. You are about to find out.

1. Sun
2. Mercury
3. Venus
4. Earth
5. Mars
6. Jupiter
7. Saturn
8. Uranus
9. Neptune
10. Pluto

The planets move around the sun in an oval path called an **orbit.** Our Earth orbits the sun just like any other planet. Our Earth year is the time it takes for Earth to orbit the sun once.

Journey Map

Here is a map of our space journey. We head straight for the sun and go as near as we can before turning and heading out toward the planets. On our way, we will see many huge lumps of rock and metal tumbling through space. These are **asteroids,** which **orbit** the sun just as the planets do. We may also see **comets.** Comets are like huge, dirty icebergs shooting through space. As they break up and melt, a tail of gas and dust, millions of miles long, forms behind them. While visiting some planets, we will also see their natural **satellites,** or moons. Moons are huge balls of rock and ice that orbit around some planets.

Mars

Earth

Mercury

Page 18

Page 10

Venus

Page 16

Page 14

Page 12

Sun

Comet

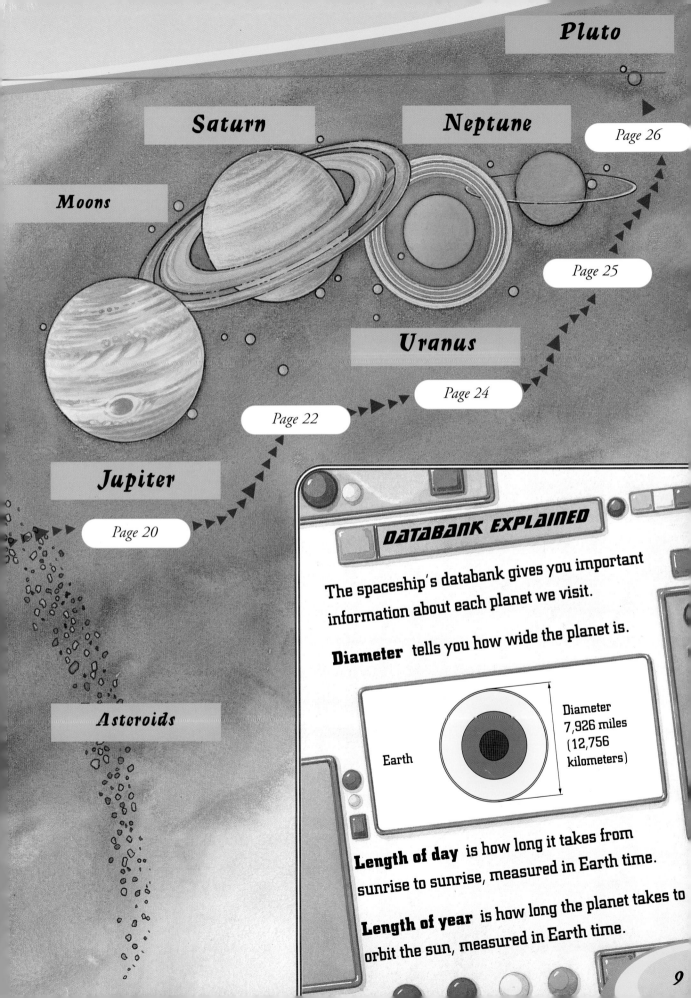

Pluto

Page 26

Saturn

Neptune

Moons

Page 25

Uranus

Page 24

Page 22

Jupiter

Page 20

DATABANK EXPLAINED

The spaceship's databank gives you important information about each planet we visit.

Diameter tells you how wide the planet is.

Earth

Diameter
7,926 miles
(12,756
kilometers)

Asteroids

Length of day is how long it takes from sunrise to sunrise, measured in Earth time.

Length of year is how long the planet takes to orbit the sun, measured in Earth time.

The Blazing Sun

Our spaceship crosses millions of miles in just a few short minutes. Temperature **gauges** go higher and higher as we approach the center of our **solar system**—the sun. It is vast—one million times bigger than Earth! It fills our protective viewing screens until all we can see is red fire.

The sun is like an immense **nuclear** explosion. Its surface is a bubbling, boiling mass of burning gases. It has been burning for five billion years. In another six billion years, it will grow in size to become an even bigger flaming ball, called a red giant. When this happens, Earth and all the other planets will be roasted and all life destroyed.

Without the sun's warmth, there would be no life on Earth. Plants use the sun's **energy** to grow. Without plants, animals would have nothing to eat.

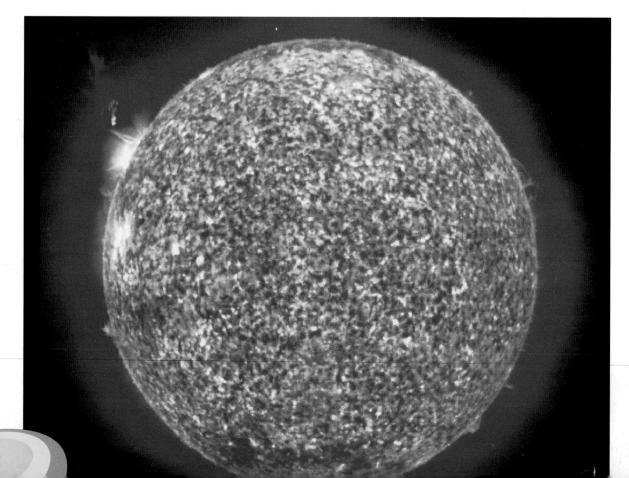

DATABANK

Distance from the Earth	93 million miles (150 million kilometers)
Diameter	865,000 miles (1,392,530 kilometers)
Size comparison	

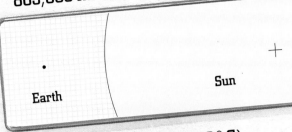

Earth   Sun

Average temperature	Surface: 10,000° F (5,500° C)
	Inside: 27 million° F (15 million° C)
Number of planets	9

WARNING!

This spaceship is fitted with protective screens. Looking directly at the sun is dangerous. Never look at the sun through **binoculars** or a **telescope** – it can blind you!

Solar flares →

Sometimes immense jets of flame **erupt** from the sun's surface and shoot out into space.

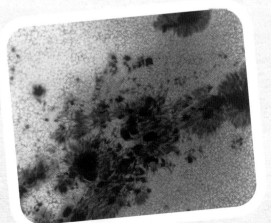

Sunspots

The sun appears to have black areas on its surface. These are sunspots, places where the surface is slightly cooler. Sunspots can be as big as Earth.

Mercury—the Dead World

*T*ouchdown! We have landed on the first of the four inner planets. Tiny Mercury is only a third of the size of Earth. It is the nearest planet to the sun. It has almost no blanket of **atmosphere** around it, to protect it from the sun's rays or keep the warmth in at night. There is never any gust of wind or drop of rain. There are no clouds or color in the sky. Even though it is daytime, we can see twinkling stars and the huge sun, which looks three times bigger here than on Earth.

A day lasts two Earth months here—two Earth months of scorching heat and **radiation**. We are glad our spaceship's **hull** can withstand the heat, which is three times hotter than boiling water. That is hot enough to melt lead! When night does come, temperatures will drop far below the freezing point.

Mercury is only slightly bigger than our own moon. This photo, taken by the *Mariner 10* **space probe**, shows it also looks like our moon.

DATABANK

Distance from the sun 36 million miles (58 million kilometers)

Diameter 3,031 miles (4,878 kilometers)

Size comparison

Earth   Mercury

Average temperature
Day: 720° F (400° C)
Night: −300° F (−170° C)

Length of day 59 Earth days
Length of year 88 Earth days
Number of moons 0

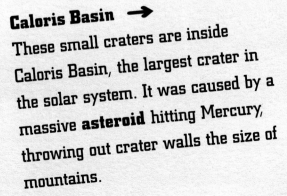

Craters

A crater is the round mark left by a **meteorite** smashing into a planet, just like a pebble thrown into sand. Mercury's landscape is blasted with huge craters made by meteorites that showered the planet millions of years ago.

Caloris Basin →

These small craters are inside Caloris Basin, the largest crater in the solar system. It was caused by a massive **asteroid** hitting Mercury, throwing out crater walls the size of mountains.

Venus—Our Savage Sister

Venus is often called our twin or sister planet. Named after the ancient Roman goddess of beauty, it is the planet closest to Earth, and almost the same size. It is also the brightest planet visible from Earth. However, there is one thing that makes Venus a very different sister—its **atmosphere**.

Venus has a cloudy atmosphere so thick it presses down on the surface like a million blankets. If we stepped outside our spaceship, we would be crushed as flat as paper. No heat can escape the atmosphere. It is like being trapped inside a huge greenhouse, with temperatures rising even higher than on Mercury. This "greenhouse effect" causes **sulfuric acid** to rain down from the violent raging storms above.

We do not stay long on Venus.

This picture of the surface of Venus is made up of many smaller photographs taken by the *Magellan* **space probe**. It spent four years in **orbit** around Venus.

DATABANK

Distance from the sun	67.2 million miles (108.2 million kilometers)
Diameter	7,520 miles (12,104 kilometers)
Size comparison	

Earth   Venus

Average temperature	864° F (462° C)
Length of day	243 Earth days
Length of year	225 Earth days
Number of moons	0

Visitors to Venus →

Four Russian Venera space
probes have landed on Venus
and photographed its surface.
It is hot, dry, and quite
smooth. Storms and high
pressure have **eroded** away
many mountains and hills.

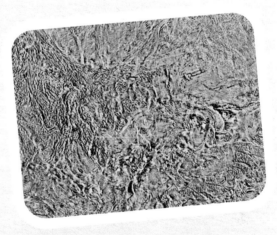

Magellan Probe

In 1990, the U.S. *Magellan*
probe sent back photos of
Venus. They showed that there
may once have been oceans on
Venus, but these boiled away
millions of years ago.

Earth—the Water Planet

Our spaceship takes us into an **orbit** around our own planet. As we circle over the Pacific Ocean, all we can see is blue water. After the violent storms we saw on Venus, Earth looks gentle and welcoming.

Earth's **atmosphere** protects its surface like a blanket from the intense heat of the sun on one side and the coldness of space on the other. If it were much colder, all the water would turn to ice. If it were much hotter, all the water would boil away. Earth is the only planet where the temperature is just right for lots of water. The atmosphere also keeps in plenty of air. It is the warmth of the sun, plus the water and air, that make Earth just the right kind of planet for living things to survive.

White storm clouds swirl in the atmosphere above Earth's surface.

Distance from the Sun	93 million miles (150 million kilometers)
Diameter	7,926 miles (12,756 kilometers)
Size comparison	

Earth   Moon

Average temperature	57° F (14° C)
Length of day	24 hours
Length of year	365.25 days
Number of moons	1

The moon

Earth's moon is a dead world, much like Mercury. It has no atmosphere and so has no air, no blue sky, no water, and no weather. It orbits Earth once every 27.3 days. Twelve people landed on its surface as part of the Apollo Program.

Seas without water →

The moon's surface is heavily cratered from **meteorites** and **asteroids** crashing into its surface. Some of these collisions were so violent they melted the moon's surface, flooding it with **lava**. These lava flows left huge, dark, flat patches that we call seas.

Mars—the Red Planet

Our spaceship breaks out of Earth's **orbit** and crosses millions of miles to approach a planet about half the size of Earth. We land on its surface and soon see why Mars is called the red planet. This cold and dusty planet is covered in red dust. Sometimes the wind whips the dust into huge, red sandstorms. In many ways, Mars is the planet most like Earth. It has a thin **atmosphere** and a day lasts almost exactly the same time as on Earth.

Out our **portholes,** we see a world quite similar to an Earth desert. The sky is pink with a few wispy clouds. The wind blows across orange sand dunes, craters, huge dead **volcanoes,** and mountains. One mountain, Olympus Mons, is the largest mountain in the **solar system**, three times higher than Mount Everest!

The spectacular surface of Mars was photographed by the *Viking Orbiter.*

18

DATABANK

Distance from the sun	142 million miles (228 million kilometers)
Diameter	4,224 miles (6,794 kilometers)
Size comparison	

Earth   Mars

Average temperature	– 81° F (–63° C)
Length of day	24.5 Earth hours
Length of year	687 Earth days
Number of moons	2

Waterworld →

Many scientists believe that millions of years ago Mars was a warmer planet and it had its own seas. Now the water is gone, but we can still see what look like dried-up riverbeds. This photo was taken by the *Viking Orbiter*.

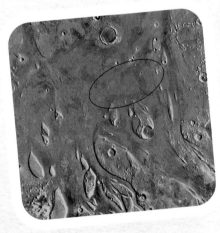

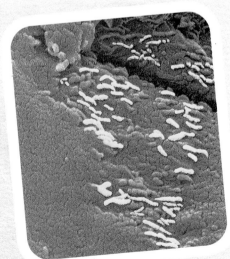

Martians?

In 1984, a **meteorite** that appears to be a lump of rock from Mars landed on Earth. Some scientists think it has tiny **fossils** of **bacteria** on its surface. Could this mean there was once life on Mars?

Jupiter—the Gas Giant

As we get nearer to Jupiter, we can hardly believe its size. It is the largest planet in the **solar system**—1,330 times bigger than Earth. Its surface is beautiful. It looks like white, red, brown, and orange paints, swirling and mixing. A giant red eye on its surface seems to look at us.

Our spaceship plunges straight into its churning **atmosphere**. We travel down through thick, white and orange clouds flashing with lightning, then into bluish, icy water droplets, and finally into gases so thick it is almost like being underwater. It gets darker and darker. Somewhere beneath us is the rocky **core**. The incredible heat and **pressure** outside are damaging our **hull**. We turn around and head for space.

Jupiter is a giant ball of gases.

Distance from the sun 483 million miles (778 million kilometers)

Diameter 88,846 miles (142,984 kilometers)

Size comparison

Earth

Jupiter

Average temperature –250° F (-157 ° C)

Length of day 10 Earth hours

Length of year 12 Earth years

Number of moons 16

The red spot

Jupiter is a planet of incredible storms. The red spot is the largest storm in the solar system. This massive hurricane, three times wider than Earth, has been raging for 300 years!

Life on Europa? →

Europa is one of Jupiter's many moons. Scientists think there may be a 62-mile (100-km)-deep ocean beneath its icy cracked surface. If this ocean also contains underwater **volcanoes**, Europa may have the water and heat needed to support life.

Saturn—the Ringed Planet

We are now in deep space, many millions of miles from Earth. A huge and amazing planet fills our viewing screens. Saturn is the second largest of the planets. It is similar to Jupiter and just as beautiful. Like Jupiter, it is a vast ball of gases with an inner **core** of rock and ice. Around the planet are huge flat rings made from lumps of rock and ice that **orbit** the planet like billions of tiny moons.

We do not enter Saturn's **atmosphere**. Like Jupiter, it is a planet of amazing storms. Winds can blow up to 1,100 miles (1,800 kilometers) an hour! Beneath the stormy surface are hundreds of miles of thick, heavy gases, ice, and water **vapor**.

Saturn is covered in hazy yellow clouds and surrounded by beautiful rings.

Distance from the sun   886 million miles (1,427 million kilometers)

Diameter   74,915 miles (120,536 kilometers)

Size comparison

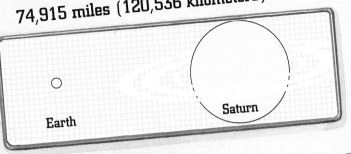

Earth   Saturn

Average temperature   –292° F (–180° C)

Length of day   10.5 Earth hours

Length of year   29.5 Earth years

Number of moons   18

Saturn's rings ➡

We do not know exactly how Saturn's rings were made. Some scientists think Saturn pulled lots of space rubble into its orbit millions of years ago. Others think a giant **asteroid** may have hit and destroyed a small moon, leaving rings of rubble and ice. Most think they may have been formed like this:

1. A giant asteroid got caught in Saturn's orbit.

2. As it was pulled around the planet, it started to break up.

3. The rings are asteroid remains that still orbit the planet.

Uranus—the Green Planet

Uranus is the third largest planet. As we approach it, we can see its eleven rings, but they are not as beautiful as the bright, icy rings of Saturn. They are very thin and hard to see because they are made from black lumps of rock and fine black dust. Dense, green-blue gases cover the planet in a thick, cloudy fog. What lies beneath this smoggy layer? Only one **space probe**, *Voyager 2*, has flown past this gas giant. We think Uranus is made from thick gases surrounding a rocky **core**. We dare not risk damage to our spaceship, so we continue our journey.

This is an artist's painting of Uranus, showing the thin rings.

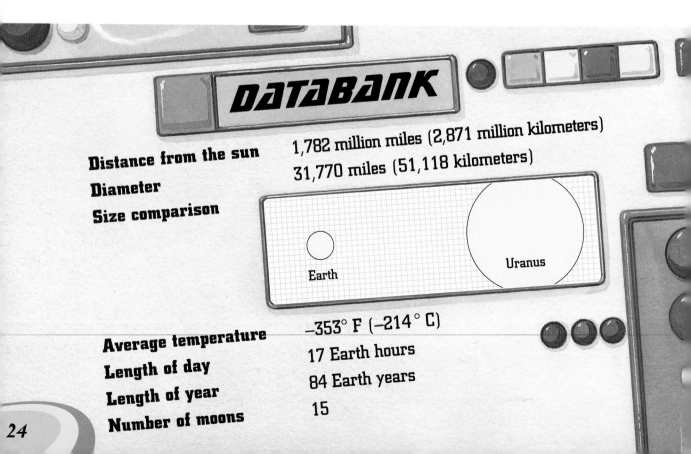

DATABANK

Distance from the sun	1,782 million miles (2,871 million kilometers)
Diameter	31,770 miles (51,118 kilometers)
Size comparison	Earth Uranus
Average temperature	–353° F (–214° C)
Length of day	17 Earth hours
Length of year	84 Earth years
Number of moons	15

Neptune – the Blue Planet

This blue-green planet is similar to Uranus. It is a gas giant and it also has thin dark rings of dust and rock. We are careful not to get too close to Neptune's surface. This is a freezing-cold world with violent storms as big as Earth! Winds here can travel at incredible speeds, up to 1,250 miles (2,000 kilometers) an hour—the fastest in the **solar system**. We see a streak of wispy clouds known as the "scooter," which travels completely around the giant planet in only sixteen hours!

Because of Neptune's blue color, it was named after the Roman god of the sea.

DATABANK

Distance from the sun	2,777 million miles (4,504 million kilometers)
Diameter	30,757 miles (49,528 kilometers)
Size comparison	

Earth   Neptune

Average temperature	–364 ° F (–220 ° C)
Length of day	19 Earth hours
Length of year	165 Earth years
Number of moons	8

Pluto—the Mystery Planet

Far away in the distance we can see Pluto, the farthest from the sun of the **solar system's** planets. It is a tiny planet, smaller than our own Moon. It is so far away that even the most powerful **telescopes** cannot discover much about its surface. We know it must be a very cold planet, covered in layers of ice and frozen gases. Some scientists think Pluto may not be a true planet but a large **comet.**

Warning signs flash in our spaceship. Unless we turn around now, we will not have enough fuel to get back to Earth. Pluto will have to remain a mystery. It is time to go home.

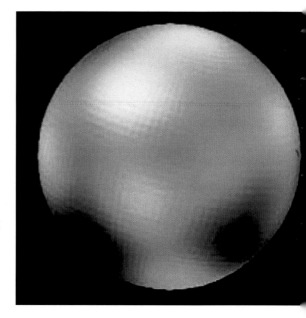

Pluto is too far away for us to photograph in any detail.

DATABANK

Distance from the sun	3,666 million miles (5,900 million kilometers)
Diameter	1,430 miles (2,302 kilometers)
Size comparison	

Earth   Pluto

Average temperature	−382 °F (−230 °C)
Length of day	6.5 Earth days
Length of year	249 Earth years
Number of moons	1

Exploring Space – Planet Probe

The spaceship we used for our journey in this book does not yet exist. All the information comes from what we have discovered using **telescopes** and **space probes**. Some of the space probes sent into space simply **orbit** planets, sending pictures and other information back to Earth by radio signals. Others are built to enter a planet's **atmosphere** and even land on the surface. The planets are so far away it would take many years and a huge amount of money to build a spaceship that could visit even the closest of planets, Mars. Perhaps a new kind of rocket power will have to be invented before humans can make amazing journeys across the solar system. People have already lived in space on space stations like *Skylab* and *Mir*. Scientists are now building a new space station that will orbit Earth. This will tell us more about how to live in space.

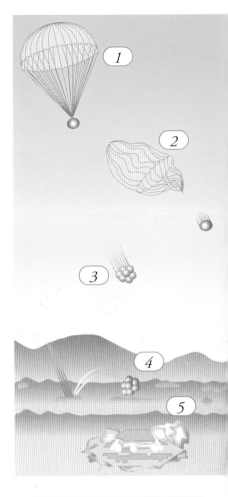

The robot Sojourner buggy landed on the surface of Mars in 1997.

1. The Mars Pathfinder *pod parachutes down to the surface of Mars.*
2. *The parachutes are released.*
3. *Large balloons inflate around the pod.*
4. *The pod bounces down on the surface.*
5. *The pod opens to release Sojourner.*

Glossary

asteroids	small planets, less than 310 miles (500 kilometers) wide, found in a belt between Mars and Jupiter in our solar system
atmosphere	the mixture of gases around a planet or a star
bacteria	tiny organisms that live in the soil, in water, and in the bodies of animals and plants, that can be helpful or harmful
binoculars	instrument with lenses for both eyes, used to make faraway objects look nearer and clearer
comet	object in space made from gas, dust and ice, that moves around the sun
core	center of something
cosmonaut	Russian astronaut
energy	ability to work or be active
erode	to wear away
erupt	to explode or shoot out material, such as hot lava
fossil	remains of a living thing, saved in or turned into rock
galaxy	one of the millions of enormous collections of stars, other solar systems, dust, and gases found throughout space
gauge	instrument for measuring or testing something
hull	the body of a ship or spacecraft
lava	hot, melting rock that comes out of an erupting volcano or cracks in Earth's surface
meteorite	small, solid object that falls from space and hits a planet with incredible impact

nuclear	related to or powered by the energy that holds the center of an atom together
orbit	path of a planet or satellite around another object in space
porthole	window in the side of a ship
pressure	weight of something pressing or being pressed
radiation	energy sent out from a source in strong waves
satellite	artificial or natural object that moves around a larger object, such as a moon
solar system	whole group of nine planets, comets, and asteroids that move around the sun
space probe	spacecraft that sends information back to Earth about space
star	large object in space, such as our sun, that is very hot and makes its own energy
sulfuric acid	thick, colorless, oily liquid used in making fertilizer that is so strong it can burn the skin
telescope	instrument that collects light or radio waves from distant objects
vapor	gas, either invisible or like mist, that forms when some substances are heated
volcano	hole or crack in Earth's crust through which lava, hot gases, rocks, and ash can escape

Space Calendar

October 1957	The Soviet Union launches *Sputnik 1*, the first man-made **satellite** to **orbit** Earth.
April 1961	Yuri Gagarin becomes the first human to leave the **atmosphere** and orbit Earth.
June 1963	**Cosmonaut** Valentina Tereshkova becomes the first woman in space.
March 1965	Cosmonaut Alexie Leonov makes the first space walk.
January 1967	Three Apollo astronauts die in a launchpad fire.
July 1969	*Apollo 11* lands on the moon. On July 20, Neil Armstrong is the first human to walk on the moon.
May 1971	The Soviet **space probe** *Mars 3* lands on Mars.
November 1971	NASA's *Mariner 9* probe orbits Mars.
October 1975	The Soviet probe *Venera 9* lands on Venus and sends back the first-ever photographs of the planet's surface.
July 1976	NASA's *Viking 1* lands on Mars.
August 1977	NASA launches the *Voyager 1* and 2 probes to explore our **solar system**, visiting Jupiter, Saturn, Uranus, and Neptune.
April 1981	The first space shuttle, *Columbia*, is launched into space.
February 1986	The Soviet Union launches *Mir*, the first permanently inhabited space station.
1986	The space shuttle *Challenger* explodes on launch.
June 1995	NASA's space shuttle *Atlantis* docks with *Mir*.
July 1995	Space probe *Galileo* launches a mini-probe into Jupiter's atmosphere.
July 1997	NASA's *Pathfinder* visits Mars, and *Sojourner* sends back photographs from the surface.
1999	Construction of the International space station begins.

Alcraft, Rob. *Space Disasters*. Chicago, Ill: Heinemann Library, 1999.

Davis, Amanda. *Our Solar System*. Rosen Publishing Group, Inc., 1997.

Oxlade, Chris. *The Earth and Beyond*. Des Plaines, Ill.: Heinemann Library, 1998.

Scott, Elaine. *Close Encounters: Exploring the Universe with the Hubble Telescope*. Hyperion Books for Children, 1998.

Sorensen, Lynda. *The Solar System*. Vero Beach, Fla.: The Rourke Corporation, 1993.

Welsbacher, Anne. *The Solar System*. Minneapolis: ABDO Publishing Co., 1997.

Index

Apollo Program 17

asteroids 8, 9, 13, 17, 23

atmosphere 12, 14, 16, 17, 18, 20, 22, 27

Caloris Basin 13

comets 8, 26

craters 13, 17, 18

day length and year length 12, 13, 15, 17, 18, 19, 21, 23, 24, 25, 26

Earth 6, 7, 8, 10, 16, 17

energy 10

Europa 21

gases 6, 7, 10, 20, 22, 24, 26

Jupiter 6, 7, 9, 20-1

lava flows 17

life forms 16, 19, 21

Mars 6, 7, 8, 18-19, 27

Mercury 6, 7, 8, 12-13

meteorites 13, 17, 19

moons 8, 9, 17, 19, 21, 23, 24, 25, 26

mountains 15, 18

Neptune 6, 7, 9, 25

Olympus Mons 18

orbit 7–9, 14, 16–18, 23, 27

Pluto 6, 7, 9, 26

radiation 12

red giant 10

rings 22, 23, 24, 25

Saturn 6, 7, 9, 22-3

solar flares 11

space probes 12, 14, 15, 18, 19, 24, 27

space stations 27

stars 7, 12

storms 14, 15, 16, 18, 21, 22, 25

sulfuric acid 14

sun 6, 7, 8, 10-11, 12

sunspots 11

temperatures 11, 12, 13, 15, 16, 17, 19, 21, 23, 24, 25, 26

Uranus 6, 7, 9, 24

Venus 6, 7, 8, 14-15

volcanoes 18, 21

water 16, 19, 21, 22